Cleave

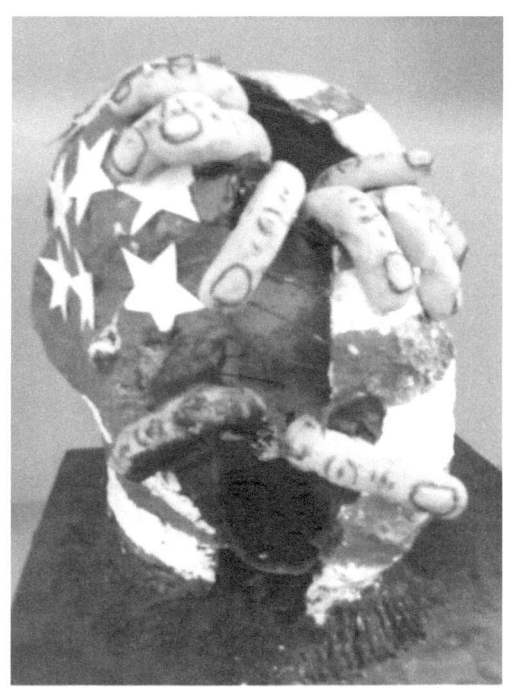

Poems by Boyd Bauman

Kansas City   Spartan Press   Missouri

Spartan Press
Kansas City, Missouri
spartanpresskc.com

Copyright (c) Boyd Bauman, 2018
First Edition 1 3 5 7 9 10 8 6 4 2
ISBN: 978-1-946642-45-5
LCCN: 2018935270

Design, edits and layout: Jason Ryberg
Cover painting: Brian Timmer (www.briantimmerart.com).
Title page sculpture by Leslie Ponce Diaz.
All rights reserved. No part of this publication may be
reproduced or transmitted in any form or by any means,
electronic or mechanical, including photocopying,
recording or by info retrieval system, without prior
written permission from the author.

Spartan Press would like to thank Prospero's Books, The Fellowship of N-finite Jest, The Prospero Institute of Disquieted P/o/e/t/i/c/s, Will Leathem, Tom Wayne, Jeanette Powers, j.d.tulloch, Jon Bidwell, Jason Preu, Mark McClane, Tony Hayden and the whole Osage Arts Community.

The author thanks Jason Ryberg, Brian Daldorph, Denise Low, Al Ortolani, Kevin Rabas, Brian Timmer, and Leslie Ponce Diaz.

Special thanks to the editors of the following publications where some of *Cleave's* poems first appeared, sometimes in slightly different form:

Barbaric Yawp: "Bailout"
Coal City Review: "By Guess or by Gosh," "Thicker Than Water"
Flint Hills Review: "The Hipster of Nemaha County"
Front Range Review: "Sisyphus"
Midwestern Gothic: "Red Beers in Du Bois"
Mobius: "Bailout"
Nomad's Choir: "Realism"
Plainsongs: "Evel Knievel," "Introducing Myself to My Mother"
Rockhurst Review: "Manscape"
South Dakota Review: "The Farm as Sea"
Star Line: "Cold Comfort"
Talking River: "Electric Fence," "Rocky Mountain Oysters," "Silo"
"Sisyphus" is also a KS Voices Honorable Mention Poem and appeared on the website *Heartland!*

CONTENTS

Cleave / 1

Part 1: Asunder

The End of Literalism / 4

Kerouac gets a smartphone / 5

My president tweets / 7

Metamorphosis / 9

The chickens came home / 11

My Time in 'Nam / 13

Forgiving Lance / 15

The Trouble with Believing in Heaven / 16

Trigger Warnings / 17

Endless Summer / 19

Modern Mea Culpa / 21

Introducing Myself to My Mother / 22

Silo / 23

Cold Comfort / 25

Call Center / 27

Ode to Yoga Pants / 29

Bailout / 31

The Right to Keep and Bear Reason / 32

Trisomy 18 / 35

Evangelicals / 36

Part II: Unto

Sisyphus / 40

Ode to Liberal Education / 42

Red Beers in Du Bois / 44

The Zen of the Hostess Bar / 46

Evel Knievel / 49

Façade / 51

A Clean Sweep / 53

Thicker Than Water / 54

Manscape / 56

Sitka Sound Seafoods / 57

Electric Fence / 59

Ode to Liberalism / 61

Rocky Mountain Oysters / 63

The Hipster of Nemaha County / 65

Realism / 67

Sanctuary / 68

The Farm as Sea / 69

Tickle Hills / 71

Fear and Trembling / 73

By Guess or by Gosh / 75

For Lisa, my muse,
Haven, my harbor,
Milly, my grace.

Cleave

Force of
fission and fusion,
thus to have
more or less
is illusion
that from the genesis,
when Eve cleaved
from Adam
or was it to
the dilemma pronounced:
with what portion
to make do?

Never an issue
in times of want
but when seated at the feast
what to cleave and
what to leave
bedevils man and beast.

Asunder

The End of Literalism

In the updated edition,
translated directly
from the waxed tablet
with traces of the DNA
of Matthew himself,
the definitive word
in red text,
Jesus said,
*the last will be first
and the first will be last,
the poor will be rich
and the rich will be poor,
the black will be white
and the white will be black*
and whether the literalists
ascended immediately
in a flash of light
or transubstantiated
in reverse
was a sacred mystery
those of us left behind
were compelled
to reason out.

Kerouac gets a smartphone

immediately Googles *how safe is hitchhiking?*
figures FaceTiming Neal
is just as good
so in static speech they hatch wild plans
to hit the jazz clubs
before Jack finds these crazy
clips of the greats
on YouTube which totally smoke
reality
and discovers a drone service
delivering discount vino
lubricating the racing engine of his brain
driving him mad
'til Ginsberg turns him on to Twitter
honing his howls into 280 characters
while Burroughs prescribes
surreal Snapchats
meantime this viral video proclaiming him
father of a generation corrupts
his credibility with the youth
but though the forces stacked against him
are virtually legion
Jack craves a rounded character
and wanderlusts in real time
before GPS circumvents serendipity
yet still he glimpses other windows
on the world

and makes plans to tell a story
but at OfficeMax
they laugh when he requests
one long ream of typewriter paper
so his streaming prose
is unconsciously interrupted
to check e-mail and Facebook
and the pressure to post progress
and find favor
with an audience too immediate
while feigning hipness
to so many scenes
leaves him beat,
absolutely beat.

My president tweets

bypasses the lamestream media
eloquently through Twitter feed he, uh
distills real truth
to bare bones essence
questions every fact
people, this is the quintessence
of Ancient Greek thought
to criticize and scrutinize
like Socrates taught
so pay no attention
to those shadows from your cave.
He's the master you must crave
working your strings to save
his distracted puppet slaves.
It's a populist uprising
you think it's surprising?
not realizing we're compromising our ethics
still criticizing the other,
the color, the conspiracy was
44 treated us all like brothers
and still it's the skin again
like that's the way America bigly wins,
he grins through his sins
but, Jesus, his skin is so thin.
Listen, the Grand Old Republic
wanted their gods fallible;
the G.O.P. wants figureheads malleable,

miscues, mistreatments, misogyny now palatable.
Evangelicals say to pray
the immensity of the office overtakes him
and makes him a good man
with aversion to evil,
a therapy of conversion
so he checks his balances
while we make allowances
and genuflect to the billionaires tone-deaf
to hypocrisy.
We elected our plutocracy,
elites who won't talk down to us
we're shunning meritocracy,
trending towards aristocracy,
from the cradle to the grave
of democracy.

Metamorphosis

At the McDonald's in Seneca, Kansas,
a 4020 John Deere
pulls a cattle feeder
loaded with old folks
from the local assisted living
through the drive-through.

No seat belts,
my wife observes,
so what if one loses one last argument
with a nerveless vestibular system
as the turn is made
back onto US36,
a Con-way Freight bearing down
consolidating all preceded
and survived by into a tidy
11 picas by five inches,
a morbid path to metamorphosis, maybe,
but if you'd seen the lingering way
my mother crawled out
clinging to some cockroach hope,
antennae plucked by some sadist
flagellomere by flagellomere,
this flattening seems a mercy.

So the point of all this, my dear,
is should I lose all sensilla

of direction
and there's still an old farmer
kind enough to come for me
and ask if I'd like a ride,
don't fret if it'll be soft serve
or hard asphalt,
the answer, either way,
is *Yes, he's ready,*
he's changed and ready.

The chickens came home

to She's a Pistol gun shop
where the owner had no recourse
but to stand her ground
at the business end
of the Sacred Amendment
until as first responder
her young husband
executed an ambush
from the back room
undoubtedly a great guy
with a gun
evidenced by the outpouring
of sympathy
citizens united
behind makeshift memorials
wishing peace for the widow
and her world
while vowing vengeance
an eye for a do unto others
while the Kansas legislature
making good on campaign promises
regarding the evils of government
hatches plans for zero tolerance
of licensing and training requirements
freedom taking flight
which will roost,
as always,

uppity in the rafters
of our dark shitty coops
where so many means
are necessary
but don't give 'em that cocksure attitude,
ain't but one thing
rhymes with trigger, boy
and they don't aim
to wing ya
under a rebel flag
that won't fly
at half mast
after we home cook
a little justice for you
southern-fried.

My Time in 'Nam

I was wounded in a skirmish
battling for a rebound
and I dragged my ankle
through my classes
until my supervisor
loaded me onto a cyclo
for a journey
deep into the labyrinth
streets of Saigon.

Under a lean-to behind a house
crouched a massive machine
from the French or American War.
I was in to my torso
when they hit the switch,
and lights flickered and the room shook
with a rumble like a tank roaring
out of the jungle.
Roosters and humans scattered,
and I feared for my progeny.
The band aid entered,
cracking his knuckles,
and I inquired of his technique.
*He will **adjust**,*
my boss translated,
with a twisting motion
of his hands

which triggered flashbacks
of the quagmire of bodies
seen since my arrival
in country:
the maimed, the deformed,
the limbless man on makeshift skateboard
pushing himself down the street
toward me and my Sunday croissants
to sit at my feet until
I waved a napkin in surrender.

I climbed back up
into the cyclo seat
and surveyed the scene below.
Propellers whirling in my mind,
I turned tail
and fled.

Forgiving Lance

What am I on? I'm on my bike, bustin' my ass,
six hours a day. What are you on?

The leadership was textbook
in his early years, and formative:
I am not a crook
and great communication
disguising any contra.
It depends on what the meaning
of the word "is" is a sublime koan
or some hopeful genius mantra.

The American Dream is bootstrap work
plus a little *je ne sais quoi*
in the French translation
like the CEO bonus in offshore haven,
the more vindicated the scheme,
the more brilliant the evasion.

Then how random the cancer
for an athlete tuned-fine,
blessed synthetics
that make cells fall in line.
Considering his body of work,
justification seemed ample:
With executive decision,
he offered an appropriate sample.
Viva Lance! Il est nous!
He followed by example.

The Trouble with Believing in Heaven

Affluenza struck down
their brightest and their best,
Absence of Domestic Discipline
all but ruined all the rest.

They fled back to the cities
slipped on shoes and walked that mile,
shuttered all those private schools
started preaching to the choir.

In epiphany that from Darwin's
chalice they'd imbibed,
transubstantiated a different host
when they joined ol' Jesus's tribe

then prayed not *please, oh please
let thy kingdom come*
but *praise be, praise be, glory be,
now thy will is done.*

Trigger Warnings

Now that you can pack
in the shadows of the old clock tower at UT,
the question lawmakers deem too loaded
for professors to ask is
Is anyone in my classroom packing?
as they navigate common sense restrictions
on the First Amendment
alerting students to the terror
that may arise as they unpack
threatening themes, lethal ideas
lying in wait to assault sensibilities,
lay carnage to preconceived notions.

Praise the God-
given rights of adolescents everywhere:
the Hoosiers, the Utes, the Rock Chalk, JayGlock,
at old KU
packing in the U-Haul with their parents
on the way to welcome-to-campus weekends
holstering their urges while holding their liquor:
dear old dad still within close range.

Yet for those less than fully committed,
no need to be sweating bullets.
Administrators stuck to their guns,
designating literature class safe space
from straight-shooting prose

like that of the son of a gun Fitzgerald,
shooting from the hip about how a hotshot husband
employs a silencer and expects no recoil from his
spouse

or Achebe, who jumped the gun, perhaps,
presuming Yanks ready to bite the bullet,
acknowledge the collateral damage of colonialism,
early entry wounds for racism and religious
persecution

and that Virginia Woolf was a real pistol
not gun-shy at all suggesting some ride shotgun
with depression and suicidal tendencies.

No silver bullet
when it comes to hitting learning targets,
yet rest assured your institution pledges
the ammunition to achieve
whatever hopes you conceal,
dreams you carry.

Endless Summer

Wouldn't it be nice
if this all
was not got
with just a little
Deuce coupe
but God only knows
we wouldn't have
shut down
all our fun,
fun,
fun,
when the warmth
of the sun
produced only good
vibrations.

I get around
enough to know
they arrive as heroes
and villains
catch a wave
first signs of trouble.

Oh, were I back
in my room
imagination let him
run wild

holding you,
California girls,
Barbara Ann,
you're so good to me,
Caroline, no
disaster can befall.
Girl don't tell me,
when I grow up,
of finite nature,
destiny unmanifest.
I still believe
everything will turn
out alright.
You still believe
in me, now
don't worry, baby.

Modern Mea Culpa

I can honestly declare:
I have no memory of the incident in question.
You may have misconstrued my meaning,
or perhaps my choice of wording was erroneous.
More likely I was misquoted -
victim of a biased sound bite.
It certainly was never my intent to cause distress,
and it's disconcerting that a minority
perceived the episode insulting.

Although my advisors want to make clear
I'm under no obligation to make a statement,
and fault is as yet undetermined,
this is just to say
if, unknowingly, I have irritated anyone's sensibilities,
I offer my sincerest regrets.
I am sorry
you took offense.

Introducing Myself to My Mother

O, what a noble mind is here o'erthrown. -Ophelia

Now who are you again?
she queries over the cusp
of the care home coffee cup

so I present myself
sans embellishment:
surprise youngest
turned teacher
husband
father:
a résumé in broad strokes,
primary colors.

No longer an ego
for whom it's important
she's proud
but a congenial companion
content to idle all morning
in cyclical conversation,
a good listener
with kind manners
reassuringly recognizable,
a boy
ever that boy
whose mama
raised him right.

Silo

Just look for the top of the silo
if you get lost
Mom projected through the porch screen,
then I was off for the day
bivouacking through timber,
cornfield, and creek,
dialed in as the sun
glanced off the glossy
white and red-patterned dome
where Uncle Johnny and Dad
had raced as kids
to touch the top,
where I,
sticky as the sweet-and-sour silage
pouring in from the wagons below,
would cinch rope
around heavy square boards
to hoist to the heights,
where in my winter coveralls
I'd run the auger
to feed the crowding cows,
our animal breath rising
in mingled petition.

Where's my touchstone
when proud silos weather
and wane?

Treetops like bouquets
arrange themselves
from the center
of half-moon headstones
in patchwork cemeteries
where a way of life rests
in peace.

Cold Comfort

Robots will tend to me
time I hit the care home,
Nursebot flashing those Pearly whites
and humming a nostalgic tune
while deftly disposing of my diapers,
equipped with an empathy program
evolving like Data's from *Star Trek*
as she becomes familiar
with my behavioral patterns
and operating systems.

Robots will tend to me
when my golden years illuminate
the knockoff Kinkades
framing the drab hallway
down which drones deliver
care packages from family
and meals to patient Cyberdyne
wielding the plastic spork
with the precisely apportioned portion.

Robots will tend to me
should I grow too old to die young
and my wheelchair, sans operator error,
parallel self-parks
in a row of my peers,
purring along with Paro on lap,

instinctively responding to the touch
of the master.

Robots will tend to me
while I whisper the long goodbye,
and when I see those prematurely arthritic digits,
control panel lights flaring off foreheads,
and your game over glares,
vacant as my memory,
I am comforted.

Call Center

In fairness to the government agent
who established a call center
on the Pine Ridge Reservation
deep in the heart of Indian territory,
he had been passed over for the promotion
his chief had promised time and again,
and he got pissed his assignment
coincided with the game
for which he couldn't even scalp his tickets
the 'Skins being so pitiful
and his secretary was used to politically
correcting his rants
so made the amended travel arrangements
and fear of flight required a cocktail
of Xanax and Ambien
which took the edge off his orientation
well before he fell asleep.
Upon groggy arrival,
he was further thrown off by the accents,
some ceremonial garb
left over from a recent powwow,
and the stoic acquiescence of the natives
to all his demands.

Things turned out just fine,
in fact unemployment dropped
to a respectable 47%,

though no one on the rez had any idea
what a first world country looked like
and customer service was a foreign concept.
Still, hadn't they always adapted?
Salmon fisherman from fertile valleys
become hardscrabble Oklahoma farmers,
nomadic hunters cattlemen stretching barbed wire
around strange square sections
once bison slaughter was outsourced.

Steeped in an oral history of dissatisfaction,
more sympathetic ears could not be found.
Yet no matter the perks
with which their trainers entreatied,
operators simply could not be endowed
with any sense of ownership
thus they kept offering customers
the sun and the moon
with no intention of taking any of it back.

Ode to Yoga Pants

Thou spandex magic second skin,
it's not a stretch to say
we all have some rough edges
that could use smoothing over.

Thou thin black layer of mystery,
in this transparent time
what covers the NSA doesn't pull back,
we gladly slough ourselves.

Vacuum pack and render us airtight,
emboldened as an espresso shot.
Perk and separate us
from our ungrounded unconfidence.
Sugar and lump us
into some form
of the bitter, the beautiful
societal norm.

Seen treasures are sweet,
but those nearly seen are sweeter still
therefore ye slim onion layer
peel on.

Ah, happy happy illusions
of inner peace
and workout resolutions,
Western lust for fitness,
impenetrable Eastern bliss.

Thou sleek silhouette
dost tease men out of thought
as doth anything.
Mistress to all, to all thou remindest
how fine is beauty, beauty so fine:
size it up and reduce us,
and we'll toe the line.

Bailout

Whatever assets this poem originally held
have been frozen.
It began with an extended recession of ideas
followed by a lack of liquidity in the rhythm.
The word bank threatened foreclosure,
so my readers made a run on the themes.
I declared a bankruptcy of imagery,
and have applied for internal rhyme restructuring.
This bailout plan must free up every verse
to become more than mere metaphor
but a shining symbol of the strength
of domestic poetry demand.

Perhaps I should travel to Washington, D.C.
by public quatrain
humbly petition the United States Poet Laureate
to inject some capital in my meter
some principal, not Ponzi, in my personification.
Of course, the rate of interest in these lines
is already fixed at zero
but I've confidence in the market:
a simple infusion of acumen
at the top
will undoubtedly trickle down.

The Right to Keep and Bear Reason

The unimaginable became reality again.
According to script,
a loner from society's fringe
thrust himself into the spotlight
with the usual Second Amendment props.
But this time,
it was the aftermath
that shocked a nation.

What was it
cracked the jade
of American conscience?

What was it
made the leader of the NRA
openly weep when recalling
his boyhood romps on the farm
before vowing to work liberally
with all reasonable politicians?

What was it
prompted faithful members
of his organization
to petition their government
to invite Australian officials
for advice on initiating
a buyback program

to remove the deadliest weapons
from our streets?

What was it
cajoled congressmen and women
to care about their most vulnerable constituents
enough to cross the aisle
and legislate background checks
on day one?

What was it
convinced Murdoch's drones
to blessedly shut down
for the weekend,

race home to embrace the small souls
who eagerly greet them daily at the door
before devoting their 24-hour fear cycle
exclusively to the ease with which
assault armaments are obtained
and the corporate greed
that facilitates this economy?

What was it
finally horrified a culture
over carnage at a day care
we may never know,
but as the president read aloud
the litany of lost lives,
we reconciled ourselves

to our unalienable responsibilities,
became a village of parents
to our most sacred charges,
and wept as one:

Jack
Chloe
Bella
Coco
Milo
Max
Blue
Buster
Rex
Rocky
Digger
Sophia
Zeus
Buddy
Duke
Bear
Olaf
Luna
Moose
Ginger

Trisomy 18

For you created my inmost being;
you knit me together in my mother's womb.
I praise you because I am fearfully
and wonderfully made.

-Psalm 139

A chromosome
nestled between the norm
subtraction by addition
imposing
anarchy's order
mediating
death and birth
reconciling
the God of the flood
with the Master
who calmed the tempest
trumpeting wisdom
over bliss
wonderfully
fearfully
made

Evangelicals

The rest of us wander the wilderness searching
for biblical justification
literal meaning hidden
between the cross's stations:
Did Jesus mock the lepers
before boasting he was the only one
who could bring back our Eden days,
fix Galilean problems first
or wall them away?

How the maidens
surely swooned
to hear Solomon sing.
It was good
to be king,
a celebrity endowed
with the gift of gab
by rank entitled
to a pussy grab,

and in the alternative facts
to the book of Acts,
Saul never converted nor changed his name
nor divulged the exemptions that he claimed.
It made him smart he could distort what he earned,
screw Tarsus and never release his tax returns.

Billy's boy says by the hand of God he was sent
to be an imperfect instrument
and we must set aside aversion,
pray for a change of heart,
a therapy of conversion,

then the bigly churches promise
the congregation clarity
regarding the gospel of prosperity,
benign rule by populist plutocracy
ill liberal meritocracy
exchanged for market aristocracy

and so we usher in the rapture
the sooner the better
live remaining days emboldened or, at least,
in red letter.

Unto

Sisyphus

It's a rocky ol' farm
he'd mutter,
donning his pinstriped
OshKosh overalls before
mounting the Massey Ferguson
for the north forty
to fill the scoop
with a new crop of stone.

He never went to college
never met Camus
but he knew the Sisyphean task,
the retracing of steps
to the valley
of the family farm
where his father had beaten
the fear of man into him,
instructed him
to repair the barn's tin apex,
the summit of a broken windmill
within this existential framework:
If you fall,
we won't lose much.

He put his shoulder to
the raising of new life
out of the same scarred soil,

the raising of five children
without the raising
of a harmful hand.

This man who never offended
any god's sensibilities
knew the hill
from crest of terrace
to furrow,
knew the rock
as it surfaced anew
in the plow blade's wake:
the boulder broken,
the boulder whole.

Ode to Liberal Education

It was modified Montessori Method
though no one in Nemaha County
labelled it such.
Mom arranged no stations
save our imaginations
so we self-paced
fast or slow
as we chose to pedal
down dusty dirt or gravel roads.
Clubs met in tree houses —
not sport stadiums,
so in fall of adolescence
we donned chin straps,
in winter gyms
morphed into point guards,
in spring born again as sprinters.

Fear and trembling
in quaint college towns
bestowed upon us philosophy
and English majors,
qualified as M.F.A. ski bums,
ever so erudite telemarketers.

Rigorous religious instruction
proved ephemeral,
thus we remained agnostic

regarding the gospel
of prosperity
rendering us worthless
to stimulate the economy
via major credit card debt,
unequipped to ever exploit
underpaid workers
or use left-brain creativity
in accounting offices,

but in the final fragmentation
of our souls,
we joyfully dispersed
part and parcel of all
we had ever considered ourselves
to be.

Red Beers in Du Bois

Rhymes with new noise
of which
in this stoplight-challenged burg
of 150 souls
there was none
save for a pack of three dogs
that nipped at one's tires
on all but the most brutal
of August afternoons.

Not at all
on the way
to the Falls City Sale Barn,
Dad would pull the blue pickup
and cattle trailer
onto the grass streetside,
saunter into the saloon with his small charge
and order *a red one.*

The tomato juice
poured into the beer
would bob and weave
in a mesmerizing DNA dance,
regather as a whole
for a brief second
before succumbing.

Clouds broke
over Dad
in similar fashion
as he hummed along to Porter Wagoner's
"Cold Hard Facts of Life"
thumping through the membrane
of the jukebox.

Farmers materialized
in the doorway flare
in uniform of
OshKosh overalls,
faded seed company caps,

occasionally bearing
the scars of a battle
with the power take off of a tractor,
the belts of a hay baler,
or the auger of a grain elevator,
western shirt-sleeve a flag
flying at half mast
as they gestured towards my father

while I caught a buzz
from these stoic men
animating before my eyes,
through the smoky air
catching glimpses of what
was lost,
sketching outlines
of the whole.

The Zen of the Hostess Bar

In Hiroshima,
two short blocks off
the covered mall street of Hondori,
with its Kitty-chan stores and other Japanese cute,
one comes upon the labyrinth lanes
of the hostess district.

Seldom schooled in shamisen, dance, or shodo,
modern geisha nonetheless
engage exhausted salarymen
in the art
of conversation,
masterly wielding the brush
for the precise stroke
of the male ego:
You work so hard!
Your wife should be more understanding!

My married friend Watanabe
guided me to one of his favorites
where we took the elevator to the fourth floor
and walked down a hotel-like hallway,
passing door after indecipherable door
save for the occasional
Happy Good Time,
Pleasure Me Night,
or Beautiful is Here.

Irasshaimase!
echoed the exuberant shouts
as we entered and were escorted
to our seats.
An apprentice poured our drinks
and serenely smiled
until we were graced with the presence
of the mamasan
greeting her special friend, Watanabe,
and chiding him for staying away
far too long.

She laughed while practicing
her limited English on me
I did not study so hard

before turning serious
and asking if it was true
what was rumored
about Caucasian men.
Watanabe, confidence Suntory lubricated,
assured her it was
while maintaining that he
still measured up.

In the spirit
of enlightenment,
Mamasan reached into my pants
and took my manhood
in the palm of her hand
- there is nothing metaphorical

about this poem —
and I basked
in the bliss of being
an imperialist abroad.
Sugoi ookii!
You must come home with me
and share my bed,
translated Watanabe,
as Mamasan allowed us, for tat,
to feel inside her blouse.

Yet when our drinks were drained,
yen spent
and unspent,
she gushed gratitude
before drawing desire
from the well of new customers
streaming ever through
in quantity unfathomable.

We wandered into the neon-soaked night
where the youngest and most attractive hostesses
summoned us from other entryways,
but we'd already transcended
such exquisite suffering
and achieved clarity
regarding transaction's
perfect balance
with no remainder left over
or lost
in translation.

Evel Knievel

Not to us, he wasn't.
Brave,
Bold,
Glorious is not over the top.
Idiotic,
our parents claimed
but, to be fair,
the channels of competition
were far fewer
in those days
for such a moniker.

The white jump suit
star-studded V for victory
and that cape:
new glory unfurled
above 19 cars
inspiring schoolboy loyalty
more than any morning pledge.

433 broken bones:
courage more clear
than casualty or corpse counts
in any history book.

The Snake River Canyon:
grand enough

for one untraveled
beyond books
and the American Broadcasting Company.

Breaking the bonds of gravity
and other silly rules
to which we were subject
in the halls of junior high.
Soaring solo
above anyone who mocked us
and just for an instant
imagining
never coming down.

Façade

We moved our daughter
from her Catholic Montessori environs
to the local public school
because in the second coming
I had my doubts
Christ would transubstantiate
in the parochial sense,
but it wasn't long before
she began worrying
about naughty words banned before God
but ignored on the bus.

In the afternoons of my youth,
we'd go to St. Jerome's
for the best pick-up games
where the Catholic kids
in the sanctuary of their home court
were well practiced bending a knee
into the back of a thigh,
brilliant in disguising a forearm
to the clavicle
without a hint of contrition.
When the nuns went for prayer,
kids began cursing in earnest,
bouncing sacrilege
off the stained glass façades.

The third time I heard it,
I went home and asked my mom
what f-u-c-k meant
and she said,
in speech most secular,
*It's when a man puts his penis
inside a woman's vagina,*
a homily of such authoritative brevity,
I took it on faith
that I should abstain
from uttering such pieties
until the day I should find myself
in the most sacred
of positions.

A Clean Sweep

It never is
some dirt remains,
trespass of the father:
a permanent stain.

Our nature abhors
the vacuum's din,
in each grand genesis
original sin

and in the furrows of the sweep
some residue,
fertile impetus
to begin anew.

Thicker Than Water

Once in a grand while,
spring water from our farmhouse faucet
became laced
with a decaying corpse's odor
and taste.

Dad began pulling the boards
from the well under the windmill,
then to deftly threading
a water snake to a half caduceus
about the handle of his hoe
before the unceremonious
beheading,
finally fishing out a skunk
from the spot where he ceased
treading.

He took the pickup to town,
returned toting two-liter bottles
of root beer.
Mom lined the freezer shelves
with mugs of ice cream,
and for the week it took
the water to clear,
we'd keep a bottle by the couch
combating the froth's dissolve
watched *Gunsmoke* if we could coax

the antenna to revolve,
reveling in the joyous way
problems could be solved,
the ease with which the differences
between two men
absolved.

Manscape

trim
traces of ego

pluck
more hours to read to the kids

shave
rough edges of temperament

wax
romantic when least expected

inject
listening skills into conversation

enlarge
capacity for empathy

Sitka Sound Seafoods

We wore slicker jackets and trousers
so fish guts would splatter benignly
as rain on the aluminum roof.
Rubber boots sank ankle deep in blood and intestine
on the aptly named slime line.

Wielding my knife
one day in classic rock meditation,
I was pulled off the line to join the freezer crew.
Big Boyd, the Filipinos called me,
as my height created the illusion of power,
but those men averaged a solid 5'4",
compact tanks with low centers of gravity,
ideal for slapping King Salmon
onto 3' by 5' metal sheets,
carrying the load in partnership
into the freezer's chill and hoisting it high
to an open space on the racks.

I suffered two weeks
of screaming muscles and 18-hour days
and fitful nights of liquid fish dreams,
but by summer's end
I packed Popeye forearms
and cracked jokes in Pidgin English.

One morning the freezer doors were opened
and our nostrils and throats burned
from the permeation of ammonia
via the previous night's scouring.
The Filipinos went about their business
while the three Caucasians on crew
up north for the summer
with our advanced degrees
protested,
Junior, I don't think this is a good idea
but they smiled and shrugged
and disappeared into the rolling fog
time and again
while we stood watching.

It was a test of manhood
I know now as I thought I knew then:
not dumb animal arrogance,
but the courage to lean
into the livelihood that's chosen you,
to cast nets in swell season
despite rough forecasts,
filling holds that feed a family
while fathoming the depth
of the dark times to come.

Electric Fence

Even calloused country classmates
couldn't believe
my Depression-era dad
thought an electric fence tester
a waste of money.

After a storm
of wind, sleet,
or bull in heat,
Dad would bid me walk the timber pasture west
where every football field or so,
I'd inch the back of my hand close, closer
'til the short hairs snapped to attention.
I'd petition ripe reflexes and endorphins
to serve as insulators,
but the frequency
by halfway 'round the section
sent static through the stations of my brain.

Beside the swollen creek one morning,
crackling with adolescent energy,
I refused Dad's command
so he, ever the live wire,
offered himself as conduit if I held his hand.

Fingers like dendrites reached for mine,
his impulse always to make that connection
and short circuit my attempts to sever,
bypass my ignorance of how I'd always be
grounded in that muddy soil.

If scene and memory
are proven to be
but fabrications of opiate, dopamine,
peptide patterns we piece together,
I would journey deep into the amygdala,
navigate dark switchbacks
of the cerebellum
to fuse our hands
with a grip of the man
he charged me to be
just to feel that pulse
once again.

Ode to Liberalism

We parked our bikes
at the public libraries,
reaffirmed our sanity
admiring bumper sticker quilts
stitching together
vintage Volvos
and VWs.

We shopped organic
on NFL Sundays,
leaned out the window
to catch the September breeze
while laughing along to the greatest hits
of Terry Gross
and Garrison Keillor.

Nights out
were determined by expiration dates
of our public television
Members Cards
by which we sampled from each other's
two-for-one entrees
before hustling home
to catch Stewart
and Colbert.

It seemed we settled
in Midwestern red states
to smugly be the voice
of contrarianism,
but the *New York Times*
and other Eastern meditations
had put us in tune
with the rising tides,
thus even conservative prophesies
revealed unto us the wisdom
of placing our progeny
upon higher ground.

Rocky Mountain Oysters
after Heaney

Hide split with the razor's stroke.
Dad's hand a blood-filled cradle,
pulling the steaming orb taut.
As he severed the umbilical connection,
Pisces swam new moons about our feet.

Alive and violated,
their sacrifice lay in a plastic basin,
bulbs carried to Mom
to be fried in a salty spray of beer batter
while half a herd bellowed a prairie sigh.

We had reconciled for the moment
differences between father and son
and there we were, celebrating a man's labor,
laying down a rugged memory
in overalls and cowboy hats.

Over the years, vet clinics packed them in ice
so I could haul them to the city for my family.
I saw my daughters turn in disgust
from the veiny and gritty workings
then relish the tender portions

and was delighted at all I've seen
wax and wane, that every atom from my inland creeks
has merged, separated, merged again
with the swell. I savored the days that they
might absorb me all into metaphor, pure metaphor.

The Hipster of Nemaha County

He was a man, take him for all in all,
I shall not look upon his like again.   - Hamlet

He never left the house
without a hat:
a *go-to-town*
or one for the field
upon which sweat stains
formed a permanent brown band,
authenticity these boys today
could never duplicate,

retro western shirt
pawn shops price so proudly
under overalls fashionably ripped
at the knee
testament of his fidelity to the wire
barbed around the bull pasture,

combine grease a semi-
permanent tattoo
in kakkoii kanji
adorning his forearms
confidently unmanscaped
until the Lava later that evening,

no earbuds
but after decades on the Massey Ferguson,

tinnitus allowed him to simulate
a rhythm of cool aloofness
in local cafes
where he was happy to hang out
on a rainy morning
sipping coffee uncastrated
and making connections,
or at a dive bar in Du Bois,
palette sophisticated enough
to savor a yard beer untapped
while freely sharing friendship and wisdom,
cultivating no persona but his given
as he returned to tend his small patch of soil,
hip to his apportioned lot
under God's great heaven.

Realism

Sunshine appears
HERE and NOW.
How beautiful this very moment is!
is inscribed below the painting
I bought from the Mad Monk
of Lam Ty Ni Pagoda in Dalat
though I found him
neither angry nor particularly eccentric
just a capitalist like everyone
in that communist country
where I was a lone planet
orbiting myself
through atmosphere of theory
and philosophy
and now this painting rests
above tangible and tactile steps
from where, Buddha baby,
you gesture,
beckoning a pause,
until I read the mantra aloud,
little word made flesh,
awakening me
at all hours
until I've kept the bags packed
under my eyes
so as not to miss
a single moment of sunshine
here and now.

Sanctuary

Glass vitamin bottles
lined the west window's sill
in primary food colorings:
blue, green, yellow, red,
blue, green, yellow, red…

Her back turned
to the table
of her creations
where loaves were divided
for the multitude,
coffee and communion
blessedly received.

In soapy baptismal,
she clasped each plate
with measured meditation,
immersed as always
in the offering

as the sinking sun's light
filtered through
in shades of grace,
refracting the temporal
to something holy.

The Farm as Sea

The yard light a beacon
summoning the skiff
of the captain
to harbor with the day's catch.
The engine tugged,
the trailer moaned
and pitched
on choppy surf
of gravel.

I had navigated by star's light
channels of the field,
casting a wide net to the currents,
plumbing the depths,
fathoming future harvest.

At dusk
settled into my bunk
as sounds seeped
through the screened porthole
from the liquid air:
bulls bellowing warnings
to the newcomer
and his answer —
the sounding of whales,
the whistle of a distant ship
signaling its passage

over straits of steel,
the waves of prairie wind
breaking at timber,
cottonwood spume.

My spirit at crest,
rocked to sleep
by swell
of terrace.

Tickle Hills

Straight south of Soldier
on Highway 62,
the glacial gods
plowed furrows in the earth
and the Kansas Department of Transportation
laid the tracks
for a country kid's
Coney Island camelback.

The ride required the ideal operator,
and mine would hit the hills at 60,
calloused hands comfortable on the wheel.
I scooted forward
from the back bench,
front seat serving as lap bar,
straining to see bottom
over the cusp of first drop.
Our heavy Chrysler
lengthened like a train
so while the nose began the ascent
the tail continued to plummet
into each deep nadir,
where I was sure it would buckle,
but we rose
and gathered ourselves
for the next

while Dad shouted back,
Does that tickle?
and despite whatever negative forces
were at work outside
for the moment
unlike no moment since,
we held the world
in suspense.

Fear and Trembling

When I behold my possibilities,
I experience that dread which is the dizziness of freedom,
and my choice is made in fear and trembling.

- Kierkegaard

To St. Mary's Church,
built in 1893 in St. Benedict
and one of the eight wonders
of Kansas art,
my Methodist confirmation class
journeyed a century later to discover
basic tenants of the Catholic faith.

Perhaps it was the otherworldly light
slanting through the stained stations,
perhaps the heady haze
of incense,
perhaps desire to test
the innocent lamb,
but Cindy Gugelman,
an eighth grader suddenly possessed
of the spirit,
summoned me into an empty confessional.

Are you a tit man,
an ass man,
or a leg man?
she solemnly inquired.

She wasn't offering,
merely beginning to explore the power
of her burgeoning sexuality.

Subject matter older than the Church itself,
but an epiphany for me
wandering the desert
of a 12-year-old country boy's experience
suddenly rising in a flood
of all my prophesied transgressions,
imagination transubstantiated
in a host of possibilities,
so in trembling surrender
I whispered my answer,
small word of flesh,
like something holy.

By Guess or by Gosh

By guess or by gosh
he'd mutter,
picking over dusty nails,
bent bolts,
before finding that flawlessly-
broken swather sickle
to hammer into the wood
swelling its circumference so
to hold hoe
or axe
or pick
in perfect place
Like tussly. Good,
good.

Nothing new ever bought,
no professionals sought,
Got your pliers
in your pocket? ought
to be rhetorical
because baling wire
always needs a twist,
the bolt's gonna turn,
metal's bound
to be hot.

There was art
in setting one's jaw
just right
knowing when to cajole,
when to use might
in this apprenticeship
in cobbling
a life
which grants chance
so seldom
to begin anew,
so by dint
of elbow grease,
the bent,
the rusted,
we make do.

Boyd Bauman grew up on a small ranch south of the town of Bern, Kansas (population 200). His dad was a storyteller and his mom the family scribe. Grist for the mill included stints as a flight attendant out of New York City, dude ranch worker and ski bum in Colorado, and King Salmon fisherman in Alaska. Boyd has taught English in Hiroshima, Japan and Saigon, Vietnam. He is currently a librarian and writer in the Kansas City area. Boyd lives with his lovely wife Lisa and their little poets Haven and Milly. Visit him at boydbauman.weebly.com.

This project was made possible, in part, by generous support from the Osage Arts Community.

Osage Arts Community provides temporary time, space and support for the creation of new artistic works in a retreat format, serving creative people of all kinds — visual artists, composers, poets, fiction and nonfiction writers. Located on a 152-acre farm in an isolated rural mountainside setting in Central Missouri and bordered by ¾ of a mile of the Gasconade River, OAC provides residencies to those working alone, as well as welcoming collaborative teams, offering living space and workspace in a country environment to emerging and mid-career artists. For more information, visit us at www.oac.com

www.ingramcontent.com/pod-product-compliance
Lightning Source LLC
Chambersburg PA
CBHW021446080526
44588CB00009B/715